FOR ME, THE WAR
BEGINS IN AN ELEVATOR

poems by
Aida Dziho-Sator

Blue Cedar Press
Wichita, Kansas

For Edo, Ema and Demir, whom I love the most.

I am forever grateful to Gretchen Eick and
Michael Poage for their encouragement
and support in writing and publishing of this
book. Without you this wouldn't be possible.
Thank you.

"Aida Džiho Sator's poetry rewards us with a rare simplicity and wisdom. It deals with our complex personal histories and collective memories, and the questions of guarding them, no matter how selective they are. Lines are hesitant, as if interrupted; they express a bewilderment of a child trying to distinguish a play from a lethal war strategy, tornado from detonation, menstruation from being wounded, hugging from clogging. The exploration of language is focused on its paradoxes and ambiguities – the war *breaks* when it *starts*, elevator is *downing* you, not *lifting* you – with a strong emphasis on imagery – a pupil is a deep *black hole*; bodies and heads – white and pink spots in a *frozen painting*. Her poetic voice impersonates and inhabits individual bodies and places of suffering, thus standing against the processes of *freezing* and *abstracting* that threaten our very humanity. Powerful in its lucidity, it questions rather than answers the most challenging ideas of wholeness, identity, self-expression and the possibility of translation. For we speak by breaking the silence, but also speak by what remains silent. Is something *broken* or *Do we break it*? *Do poems eat words* or *Do words eat poems*?"

~Ivana Maksic, a Serbian poet

Table of Contents

THE WAR LIFE

WHAT WE DO WITH OUR PAST

My sister's memory of our childhood
Is bad
That's what she says
But I think
It's just selective in different ways than mine

She told me to guard them
Our memories
Since
We've been together from the start

And I do.

GOING DOWN

For me, the war begins in an elevator.

Two boys and I are going out to play outside.
Other children are already out.
They're playing.
They're all new friends. They are new.
I am new. I'm eleven.
We are all new to this place.
The apartment building is new.
The elevator.
We've never been lifted so many times a day.
We would be faster running.
But it's all new.
We can't miss the ride. The doors are yellow.
We run inside. The inside walls are pink.
The buttons are round and numbery and fresh.
They want to pop out.
There is a mirror.
It reflects the pink of the walls and the tops of our heads.
We are barely tall enough to see our faces.

The youngest boy isn't.
He jumps and laughs. With his tongue out.
And then we are shaken.

We shake and now we are all jumping.
We don't know what's happening.
We scream out guesses.
Tornado? We don't have them here.
Is it broken? Did we break it? It's brand new!
The building is brand new.
And we are... Is it shaking?

Where's my sister?
We stretch out our hands.
We hold on to the walls.
The younger boy is smaller.
He bends his knees and is looking up. We look like a
    spider's web.
We look abstract. Or surreal. I can't tell.
I see how their faces turn from laughter to fear.
Their faces are white spots on the pink walls.
I see the eyes of the taller boy. The brown in the ..
eyes is disappearing.
The look becomes stiff.
The pupil becomes a deep black hole.
The iris is becoming more elaborate.
It is stretching and loosening, making an intricate web.
Another web. I'm thinking it wants to come out.
It wants to eat us or freeze us. I can't tell.
My stomach is twisted. It becomes a ball. Heavy.
The pink of the stomach becomes the pink of the walls.
Not brown like the eyes.
Like the poop. Will I poop?

But the intestines are not neatly going down. Like in
    the picture.

They are scrambled now. Like the eggs my mother makes.
But not yellow like the doors. They're pink, like the pink
    of the walls.
Not yellow like the pee. I think I will pee.
We stop now. We are stopped.
We are alive. The web undoes itself.
We are not a frozen painting.
We are not a scream. We are not abstract.
We go out. The other children are out.

They are lying down on the ground.
My sister is under a car. A red car.

She crawled under.
There is a red spot above her eye.
She is not all red. She is not bloody. It's just a scratch.
The windows are broken. The parents are out screaming.
Mother is calling our names. They are alive.
Everyone looks confused.
The fear is big. I look at them.
The iris from the boy's eyes is now upon all of us.
It is hugging us. Or clogging us. I can't tell.
An hour passes.

They say it was a detonation blast. First one. Ever.
You don't die from detonations.
Unless you're too close.
Windows break. Glass falls.
Elevators shake. Buildings shake.
Yellow and pink become black.

They die in a well of the black of the pupil of a child.
They fall. I fall. They break.
The war breaks. It's how it starts.

In an elevator that is going down,
that is downing you, not lifting you,
that is shaking you,
that is making you abstract,
abstracting you,
enveloping you in an iris of the frightened look,
freezing you, breaking you,
pink by pink,
blast by blast,
death by death,
day by day.
The war for me begins in an elevator.

SIBLINGS

We are driving up north
To our uncle's
To where it's safe
For now
To escape the war
Even though dad said there wouldn't be a war
He watches all the news
All the time
He must know
And his friend came
To say it was going to be a war
And he said no
We can't be enemies
It's just not right
his mind refused
But then it blew
The detonation was strong
And I could have died
You could have died
And we sit in the back
Of our red Lada
Quarrelling over

Who's to sit in the middle

And how you didn't pee
And how I didn't poo
How you left your doll
And I my new shoes
Never thinking
We could have died
On that day and,
That we were almost going to die
For so many times
In the years to come

But we don't
In the end
You see
And today we sit
And talk
How we would like
For the hyaluronic lotion fillers
To become affordable and cheap
When we are 45

PERIOD

Its shelling, heavily
And we are curled in the hallway
It's the safest place to be
When they hit with grenade launchers

They come from above

It's different when it's tanks
We'd have to run to the basement
 or my cousin's small room
the one without a view
The only room without the view
In a building that is all about the view
Of the river below
Now the building is all ugly, riddled
Like Swiss cheese
But now I'm hungry
When I think of cheese
And I can't be hungry again
We don't eat that much
Food is scarce, meals are small
And now I think of chocolate

Shit, it's getting closer
I've never really been a chocolate kid
More of a sour candy stuff

And my stomach hurts

And I think why?
And I tell mum

And now the shells are here
The building's hit
And we scream
And then it stops
And we stop screaming
And I go in the bathroom
And there is blood
On my panties
And I call for mum
I think I am hit
Or something in me burst
From detonations or fear
She says it's Okay
I'm not hurt
And it's strange
I hate my body, but I'm sort of happy
For now, I will not be
the only girl among my friends
Who doesn't know
What a PMS is

WHEN THEY ALMOST KILLED ME

I am in the hills
There's a lot of us
We're collecting the wood
For fire
And it starts shelling
But it's far away
We pay no attention
I tell them to cut thorn trees
Not pomegranate
We will want the fruit
If we are alive by then
Shelling is now closer
But just one round
Some people leave for shelter
I see then the abandoned vineyard
Dried out
And I go there
Shelling is almost here
Everyone runs away

But I think I have time and they will stop

Because there are no more houses
To shell at this end
They hit houses and backyards
Where people are

Not fields and hills
It's a waste of grenades
But they do this time
I'm in the field
Alone

My aunt by now running after me
Because I wasn't back home
With everyone else
Shouting my name
Screaming to hide
I'm plucking this tree
With no life in it
It will burn nicely
I hear her yelling
And I hear the round of shelling
Is getting closer

Is coming here
But now it's too late
And he can see me
It's only me there
In the fields
And he decides to fire
And kill me

And I hear it swooshing through the air
And I lie down on the ground
Thinking I'm dead

I hear a thud
It throws me a bit
And there's dirt
And I see a hole near me
And I'm alive
It was a dud

My aunt hugs me, yells, hugs me again, and we go home.

THE COMMON LIFE

HOW THEY NEVER TRANSLATE

With feet on the table
And view of my bookshelf
White wine
Dry
Naomi Shihab Nye, Adrienne Rich,
Harryette Mullen,
And yes, Keats and Yeats, Eliot and all
The mood is set

I start the work
And I type and type
But it doesn't do

I'm struggling for words
They come and go
None of them
ever sufficing

I'm translating my poems
You see
And they're fighting it
In fear
They're going to be stripped of all meaning
Shattered and never whole
Not knowing each other
Like strangers in lines
Confused
And in anguish
Sitting like beggars on sidewalks
With empty gazes into the past they once knew

When finally, one of them
Not even the best one,
Not intimate
Not ever published
Said enough,

You stop
Write others and leave us be

It's late and I wonder,
Do poems eat words?
Do words eat poems?

It's late and I fall asleep

I GO

When I remember my divorce
I see myself as an umbrella
Me opening
Them, closing it
Them is everyone
My parents and his
He
Our child
Some more and some less
In this way or that

the sounds are
swoosh
and flap
and click
and then again
swoosh
and flap
and click

I spread
They close

And so on and on

And in one instant
I almost unhook
From myself
My mind looking a way out

But I never unhook
I stay
Sane

I take my daughter
And a few things
I look at myself in the mirror
My head ponding
Eyes so green
With tears
Watery
My black limbal rings
Hold the iris
So it doesn't spill
And I drown

I say to myself
You're beautiful when you cry

And I go

AND THAT IS WHY I LEAVE YOU

You are passive
Possessive
And a pussy
And you are just a prick
In the end
As well
You shit
And oh,
How it's
Good
Just feels so right
To curse
In poetry

TWO WOMEN WERE SITTING ALONE ON THE BEACH

You asked me if I liked figs
I said I did,
But only cold
Like yogurt
I also told you I loved
Portuguese jazz
you said you loved
flesh-coloured lipstick
and when the sun surprises you
in the morning
when it breaks through
densely lowered blinds
and falls over the dust
in the room
and they fly together beautifully
Then we talked a little about life
work and children
And how the sound of waves
Crashing over sand
collides
With the sounds of stewed vegetables
On the pan

and that neither you nor I know
which of the two
should be celebrated

LOOKING BACK

I find my photo
From 2008
And I think
I should lose a few pounds
But then I see another one
Where we eat pizza
And look happy
And I make one
I'm still good
We're still good
It's OK

GROWING APART

We don't lose us in a day
Or in a year
It takes time
Not spent together

I stop coming by
To laugh together and cry
To see if you will ever stop by
But you don't
And we are not done
But it's maybe when it starts

We start growing apart
Coffees not had
Days not shared
And I must have done
something as well
it's how it is
with people

And resentment slowly builds
You say you love me
And I you
But now I don't believe you

I hope
We haven't lost us now

A DIARY ENTRY FROM A FAIRLY SUCCESSFUL WOMAN

I wake up
I get up
I pee
I take my pills
I make coffee
Not always in the same order
And I put on makeup
I wake up the child
Wash, pee, eat
Get dressed
Sometimes we are as cute as in the commercial
Today we both yell
I leave him at school
I try to unlock the office with my car keys
I click and they just stare at me
I turn on the computer and the A.C., open my emails
I'm going to have breakfast
I'm alone today
I have an exam, then a lecture,
I go to the supermarket

I spend fifty-four marks
I go back home
Because I didn't bring my laptop
to listen for half an hour
of some meeting
Which I wasn't at, because I was at another one
To write a paragraph of the project

I start the washing machine,
I hand wash collars
I put rice and chicken in the oven
I wash my hair
I'm listening to that meeting
I hit the soccer ball several times
Against the corridor wall
I go to the dentist
I broke a tooth
Because I'm clenching my jaw
He says good morning,
So why are you always in a hurry?
I laugh
My jaw hurts
From having my mouth wide open at the dentists'

I come back, pick up the child from soccer
practice
We have lunch, the rice is overcooked
I sit down and watch an episode of a TV show
Then I play soccer
Around the house, with my son
I accidentally hit the ball into the lamp
And his Legos plane
We both laugh
Then I go to pick up my daughter from school
She eats and tells me of her day
She says she wants to go to Prague
I say we will go
We are doing homework
We learn letters
I say why can't you do something
We argue
You say you are tired
I say shut up

You tell me you love me
And you send me a gif
While taking dishes out of the machine
Because you know it's your fault

I do more around the house
We laugh

I lie down to sleep
I scroll aimlessly
I close my eyes
just about to fall asleep
and I think
oh, fuck
the laundry!

WHEN I AM OTHERS

THE BEACH
To Alan Kurdi

I was hundreds of millions of small grains
And I have lived hundreds of millions of long years
And I caressed happy faces, and birds
And the sun and small events
Big days and rain and air
And cloths, beach towels and bikinis
and then the small cells of a small body
in the darkness
Of that day
One day in the millions of days of my existence
Cold, horrible, ripped apart, escaped from time
And I caressed the little hands
that unwrapped the day before me
And the lungs and eyes and nose and fingers
And rocks and millions of minerals
That held the darkness within themselves
And every scream and every trace of
happiness
Taking him deeply under the sea frost
Where cuttlefish and sea stars and red corals
Sang him lullabies

Where planktons cried
And filled the sea with their tears

And oceans that spilled over
from their howling sea beds
And I cried
From my womb
Ow, ow, ow…
To the skies, to the heavens, to the God
I screamed...
On that day
I was a beach
and a death cloth swaddling
millions of his small shut body cells
on that day I was a beach
and I died
with him

THE DAY OF THE YOUTH

I am Ozren.
The mountain.
From my green karsty greenness,
From my leafy chest
the heavy lead flew.

I am a shrapnel.
I was painfully separated
from my leaden wholeness
and as a small, black, thorn
with pointed, angry, irregular edges
I pierced the skin and then muscles,
and then the heart
I bathed in her warm blood.
I cried for her silken,
young body that I shattered.

I am street concrete.
The blows hurt me,
sharp with iron,
they hurt my body.
My flat, lifeless plain

My gray, lifeless grayness

Their crying was my sore.
I have no name.
I'm just young
and beautiful and I stand now
on the pile

and I'm spinning on the dervish's hat
in his dance
at the end of the mind, distraught
And asking him to hoot
hooo
hooo
So that all the gates would open
golden and green
So I kneel before them and pray
To turn back the day
To turn back the clock
so that the concrete is no longer red
so that the shrapnel is no longer wrenched and
alone
so that the lead is back on the mountain
So that I am not...
So that I am...
So that I am youth again.

STRANGE MEETING

Once, I was a bullet

There was a large red puddle on the floor
They were all red
and their comfortable sneakers
Were red as well
And gauzes and scalpels and white coats
And a scream outside that I picked up with me in a vacuum
was also red and stronger than the vibrations of life in
Frightened, and crazed veins
And it all kind of flowed
Around me and by me
And I was hidden
So well hidden
A small piece of lead
Not at all brave
In that riot
A ripped apart purple
Phantasmagoria
In that crazy quest of theirs
To find me
Amidst collisions of amino acids, microbes, glycerol
Freed forms of body liquids
I was just small and hidden
Right there

Where the small intestine and pancreas meet

and I was shivering and crying

I was a bullet once
And I felt so alien
and guilty

ONCE I WAS A BRIDGE

And oh, how beautiful I was
I was so slender
My dress was white
and the skin so smooth and shiny
and I got prettier with age
with wrinkles
freckles from the sun
and traces of time
I was smiling
Every day
For hundreds of years
And people were passing by
Carried over me
Their bags, loads,
Shadows, dreams, happiness, and pain
Upright
And I just kept them safe
The river flowed below me
Wild, crazy, green, and crystal clear
I always told her she was wonderful
with wrinkles
freckles from the sun
and traces of time
I was smiling

Every day
For hundreds of years
And people were passing by

Carried over me
Their bags, loads,
Shadows, dreams, happiness, and pain
Upright
And I just kept them safe
The river flowed below me
Wild, crazy, green, and crystal clear
I always told her she was wonderful
Both crazy and in love
And we laughed out loud at each other
Haha haha hah ha

And did so for hundreds of years
And then the shadow came
One day
And stayed a long time
Neither she was green, nor I was white
And then came some noise
Through me and her
And people were passing by
They were no longer ordinary
There was pain in them
And horrified looks
And they were bent
And then the pain,

so strong
hundreds of blows to my body
oh, oh, oh
And I just broke down
In hundreds of scattered pieces
And pebbles
And my lace spilled
And together with it
countless steps that had walked over me

The river stopped at that moment
stunned in silence
and rushing upwards from my falling body

she flew into the air
she, me, and millions of our memories
human footsteps
and then she just let go
arms outstretched
and into her depths from that fear
she hid me

*To the Mostar Old Bridge that was built in 1566 and
torn down in 1993 by the Croatian Military Forces
during the war in Bosnia and Herzegovina.*

APRIL CHRONICLES

In the land of liberty and dreams
In April, one city lost its tea party
under the attacks of the recent type of warfare.
Is it fair to say that there are Boston's Markale now?
It's not.
In a country on the crossroads of the worlds
the first massacre was committed in April.
Is it fair to say that I find it harder?
It is.
A pressure cooker full of nails
Or a barrel full of explosives.
Rolling down the hill.
Oh, how the letters just roll
anger, rhetoric, terrible devices
for wine and boiled chicken wings
from mine to someone else's
point of view.
In April, in a the perfectly humane conditions of a Zoo
a seven-year-old lioness died
from Escherichia coli.
She told me she was unhappy,
And that she wanted to know the scents of the steppe,
And that her dream was freedom.
Was Africa.
And that our destiny does not affect her.
At all.
She also told me to tell the lion
that she was sorry he was left alone.
"We will always have Sofia,"
she added quietly.
In April, a woman in her thirties,
and before as much…

With big green eyes
pretty,
heavy with her big round belly
bathed a restless child
And she went to the hospital to give birth to
another.
A four-pound baby.
A Sister. My sister. Amela.
And despite all the madness of the world
In all the Aprils of the time
April
in my eyes
will always be
just hers.

FRIENDS

I saw your brother and mother this morning.

Where?

In front of your house.

How?

A sniper.

How are they?

She turned gray, and he was cleaning his rifle.

And I sit here with you in this heat
in a concentration camp.

Yes,
have a smoke. This will pass too.

PTSD

This morning I broke a mirror
It didn't show the happiness I wanted to see
And it's not like I shattered my reflection immediately
First, I tried nicely: I took some of the drowsy memories
Red cherries from the neighbor's orchard, first day of school,
The day my wife went into labor
The day the glassy rain laughed through the scents
  of lime-trees in our yard
The day I felt Alma's first upper left tooth
Under my right forefinger
And the day we all danced at Dino's wedding
I took all of that
But the brush...
The brush drew something else
Over my deep face lines, it drew the trenches we
  walked through
Over my cheekbones, the mountains we let the bloody
  kites fly from
Over my eyes, the expressions on the faces of the
  leaving friends
And me
Hanging between those two worlds
Hooked on some supernatural nail

And this has been the fifth day
I've been looking myself in the new mirror
In the hallway, right next to the main door
And this morning I just broke it
My wife looked at me
As on that very first day...

And said
Come on, we'll pick it up later
the coffee's getting cold

AN AD

I'm selling memories,
   A total of forty-five years.
Fifteen of them are well preserved, plus
eight years of pure happiness.
I give the rest not to separate them ...

They can be traded,
   for three seedlings of sour cherries.
I dreamed last Wednesday that they would bring me happiness.

CEMETERY NOTES

DEATH

I often think of death
I'm afraid of the finality of it all.
Just the cut,
Worms and the dark

But then I think of eternity,
The vastness of it,
The dull dragging of days
Surely at some point
The infinity of it all
And I'm equally
Struck
With horror

FUNERAL BLUES

She doesn't attend funerals
People die suddenly
And she cannot cancel her online EFL classes
Just like that
Suddenly
It has to be in advance
And people don't die that way
The company is strict
And she has to pay for every cancelled class
So funerals cost her

She is also uneasy with sadness
And loneliness
Not comfortable with crying
And funerals are sad
And lonely
She stays home
Teaches little Chinese children
greetings in English
and numbers and colours
She smiles all the time
And later
cries alone
For the dead

LINKS

I'm driving to my aunt's funeral
It's up north
There's snow
But not fully covering
Roads and
Tree branches
It's melted somewhat
It's now more like cotton on cotton trees
Of the American cotton fields
Vast
In the south
I saw in the movies

I haven't left enough milk in the fridge
For my daughter to drink
When she wakes up

We arrive

SYNDROMES AND SYMPTOMS

I've been diagnosed with Manier's disease
And my husband's voice
When we are not arguing
And when it's extravagantly high
Is incredibly low
And he eats some of the syllables
Away
Sometimes
Of the words he says
And I resent him
For not being sure
if I'm going mad
Or deaf
Or dead

PRAYERS FOR THE DEAD

In my country
People can sometimes skip birthdays and baby showers
Weddings and the such
But never funerals
There's some solemnity in them
Collective sadness
Over the dead
And that moment of forgiveness
Because we forgive everything
To our dead
We repeat three times
I forgive
I forgive
I forgive
In a foreign language
Of the prayers
We say
At the end

And there's also that strong feeling
Of relief for being alive
And that light chat over coffee
In a coffee shop

Because you don't go straight home
After the burial of the dead

A WOMAN WHO LOVED ORCHIDS

I dreamed of you last night
You were in a hurry and you were walking towards me
But you didn't see me
Your forehead was just as high
and your hair was just as shiny
a few grays
Hair parting on the same side
My heart stopped!
It's you!
I hurried towards you
To hug you
But then the dream became cruel,
unreal
You became two women
Who just looked a lot like you
And they looked much younger
I ran after them anyway
To tell them, to explain to them
To ask them
If they will let me touch their faces
and hug them
Because maybe it'll be the same
as if it were you

GRAPHIC CONTENT
FROM THE HOLY LAND

AL-MAGHAZI

Mornings are not sweet here
No smell of brewed coffee
In the mornings we bury our dead
One prayer for seventy of them all
Today, all together
They look peaceful under the white shrouds
One next to another
As if no one disturbed them.
Mornings are not sweet here

CONTENT SENSITIVE: SEE WHY
(see reel)

She may be 12
The rest is buried in rubble
She's covered in dust I see half her body

Blood on her face
Big round eyes
She moves her hand
And people dig around her
With their hands
She shudders, she doesn't cry
I can't see her right hand
I wonder about her legs
Will she ever walk
But I'm glad she's alive
There's hope
At least
Until another bombing
Tomorrow
But not for the boy
I see just now
On her right
Tinier than her
Half buried
And dead
So small
And alone

See reel
And
cry

ABOUT THE AUTHOR

Aida Dziho-Sator, PhD, is professor of English Literature at the Dzemal Bijedic University of Mostar, Bosnia and Herzegovina. She has one book of poems published, *I'm Waiting for the Osman's Story,* (Cekam Osmanovu pricu). Her poems have been published in *Castello di Duino Poetry Collection* in Italy, *Balkan Literary Herald, Pitchwise, The Death Project,* and the literary magazine *Life,* one of the oldest and most acclaimed literary magazines of Bosnia and Herzegovina. She is the recipient of a fellowship to the U.S. Institute of Scholars and several teaching grants in Europe. She lives in Mostar, BiH with her husband and two children.